WHAT READERS ARE SAYING...

"If you are tired of the same old advice on how to prepare for, conduct, and manage your own personal career/job change, *I Hate Mondays* is a MUST read for you! Renee walks you through how to think about changing your job/career step by step. From discovering the initial questions you should begin asking yourself, to learning how to create a resume the RIGHT way and land the job, Renee guides you through insider knowledge on the processes of interviewing, showcasing your talents, and resignation. There is zero doubt that the secrets she's learned in her years of executive recruiting will radically transform your perspective of job searching. If you want to differentiate yourself from those you are competing with on the career ladder, read and study this book!"

Michael Gionta, Founder and CEO of TheRecruiterU.com, Author of *Double Your Placements & Double Your Revenue in 121 Days or Less!*

I Hate Mondays is an excellent resource for any individual embarking on a job search! Frequently, you will hear people associate job searching with negativity, but the practical and easy-to-implement strategies offered here are bound to lead applicants to positivity. Life is too short to hate Mondays. It is time to get on the path to finding meaning and passion in what you do, and this book is a wonderful starting point!

McKenna Pfeiffer, Assistant Director, University of Wisconsin-River Falls Career Services

"This is one of the best job searching books I have read in a very long time. It keeps the interest of the reader, provides new ideas on how to stay focused on your goals, and is easy to follow."

Melissa Wilson, Director, University of Wisconsin-River Falls Career Services

"Wow! *I Hate Mondays* is an easy-to-understand, simple-to-use guide. I love her client's story and everything I learned from their interaction. I will definitely be passing this to all of my friends who hate Mondays."

Amanda Johnson, Founder of True to Intention, Author of *Upside-Down Mommy*

I HATE MONDAYS

A Guide to Landing a Job that Makes You Jump Out of Bed

by
Renee Frey

I HATE MONDAYS!

A Guide to Landing a Job that Makes You Jump Out of Bed

Published by
TalentQ, Inc.
Hudson, Wisconsin

www.TalentQ.net

Copyright © 2017 *by Renee Frey*

Cover Design by Dan Mulhern Design
Interior Design by Dawn Teagarden

All rights reserved. No part of this book may be reproduced or transmitted in any form or by any means, electronic or mechanical, including photocopying, recording, or by an information storage and retrieval system without written permission of the publisher, except for the inclusions of brief quotations in review.

Disclaimer: The Publisher and the Author does not guarantee that anyone following the techniques, suggestions, tips, ideas or strategies will become successful. The advice and strategies contained herein may not be suitable for every situation. The Publisher and Author shall have neither liability nor responsibility to anyone with respect to any loss or damage caused, or alleged to be caused, directly or indirectly by the information in this book. Any citations or a potential source of information from other organizations or websites given herein does not mean that the Author or Publisher endorses the information/content the website or organization provides or recommendations it may make. It is the readers' responsibility to do their own due diligence when researching information. Also, websites listed or referenced herein may have changed or disappeared from the time that this work was created and the time that it is read.

ISBN: 978-1975607036

Printed in the United States of America

www.TalentQ.net

*Dedicated to all the frustrated job seekers...
May you obtain a pay raise and promotion...
And LOVE your Mondays!*

ACKNOWLEDGMENTS

I'VE ALWAYS DREAMED about writing and publishing a book from a young age. I have to thank all of the teachers, professors, and distinguished authors of all the books I've read who inspired me to believe anything is possible.

First and foremost, thank you, Dustin Frey, for being my devoted husband and supporting and encouraging me in everything I do. You are my rock, love me unconditionally, and allow me to live the life I have imagined. Thank you, Aubrey and Elena, my daughters, for your smiles, hugs, and motivation, which give me purpose.

Thank you to my parents, siblings, Dustin's family, and the extended family who love me for who I am and continue to believe in me. I'm tremendously grateful for your love and support.

Every book needs an excellent editor. A special thank you to Amanda Johnson, of True To Intention, for teaming up with me to finish this book. Your guidance helped me weave an engaging story into what could have been very boring content. Your encouragement and collaboration allowed me to have a finished product. You are a delight to work with and make the process enjoyable!

A tremendous thanks to all my cherished friends, TalentQ team players, business associates, mentors, and coaches. You make me a better person and challenge me, and your encouragement keeps me going.

Special acknowledgment and a heartfelt thank you to members of our Forward Group. You help me grow, think differently, and are always there for me. I cherish you!

Finally, a huge thank you to all the job seekers and hiring managers I've worked with for allowing me to use my signature strengths every day in a profession I love and am passionate about!

CONTENTS

11 Introduction: You Can Stop Hating Mondays

19 Chapter 1: I Want More

25 Chapter 2: I'm Outta Here

33 Chapter 3: I'm Looking Good

65 Chapter 4: I'm On the Hunt

77 Chapter 5: I'm Putting Myself Out There

83 Chapter 6: I Want a Fit for Me

89 Chapter 7: I'm Ready to Impress

105 Chapter 8: I'm Showing Up and Standing Out

111 Chapter 9: I'm Sure About What I Want

115 Chapter 10: I Got It

119 Conclusion: Love Your Mondays...
         and Every Other Day

121 A Special Invitation from Renee

123 About Renee

INTRODUCTION

YOU CAN STOP HATING MONDAYS

> *"The only way to do great work is to love what you do. If you haven't found it yet, keep looking. Don't settle."*
>
> ~ Steve Jobs ~

IT WAS SUNDAY evening, and Jennifer sat comfortably in her favorite loveseat in the house, her happy place. She was reveling in the wonderful, relaxing weekend she just had, sighing and snuggling deeply into the soft leather. Not one minute of Jennifer's weekend was devoted to work and her job didn't even cross her mind. She felt completely recharged, refreshed, anew. A warm calm had taken over her body, a complete state of Zen. And then...

Oh no! I have to go back to work tomorrow!

Her stomach started to churn, and her shoulders tightened with anxiety.

I wish the weekends were longer.

Next week's tasks began to make Jennifer's mind race. Hundreds of emails would be waiting for her in the morning and there were numerous meetings on her calendar that she didn't even know if she was prepared for.

I hate Mondays!

The thoughts spiraled out of control and pretty soon she wanted to crawl under a blanket and pretend she never had to work again.

Jennifer is not alone.

Those dreaded feelings we call "Sunday-night Blues" are real. The hesitation to go back to work on Monday is not a joke. In 2015, a poll from the career site Monster.com found that 76% of American respondents report having Sunday-night blues.* Let me repeat that data: 76%! You certainly are not alone.

Work is an enormous part of our identity. The definition of the word "Career" from Merriam-Webster is: "a job or profession that someone does for a long time." The phrase "a long time" sounds daunting, doesn't it? We need to work to live. We need to make a living to support

---

* http://www.monster.com/about/a/red-white-and-mostly-blue-monster-data-shows-that-the-us- continues-to-suffer-the-most-from-sunday-night-blues

ourselves. To buy the basic necessities of life — food, housing, clothing — and to purchase the non-essential extravagant items such as dinners out, fashion clothing, accessories, tech gadgets, cars, vacations, extracurricular activities for our children, and so much more.

If you work in a full-time, salaried position, the standard in the US is typically 40 hours per week. In reality, according to Gallup, adults employed full-time report working an average of 47 hours per week. That's 20% more than the standard.

Average Hours Worked by Full-Time U.S. Workers, Aged 18+

In a typical week, how many hours do you work?

	Employed full-time
	%
60+ hours	18
50 to 59 hours	21
41 to 49 hours	11
40 hours	42
Less than 40 hours	8

Based on Gallup data from the 2013 and 2014 Work and Education polls, conducted in August of each year

GALLUP
http://www.gallup.com/poll/175286/hour-workweek-actually-longer-seven-hours.aspx?g_source=average%20hours%20worked%20weekly&g_medium=search&g_campaign=tiles

That is 28% of your time in one year spent working! Nearly ⅓ of your time. Plus, we all know that some weeks we exceed those 47 hours, which drives the percentage up even higher. Expand that in one year, and you will work around 2,444 hours. And *that's* in a perfect world.

So if we have to be devoting nearly a third of our lives to an activity, why do we settle for jobs that make us hate Mondays?

The reality is that the words "Job Search" and "Looking for a New Job" evoke negative emotions in most people. In fact, after conducting word association with a small group of people, we were shocked with what we uncovered.

We wrote the words "Job Search" on a whiteboard and asked people to shout out words that immediately came to mind. Here's what we heard:

- Anxiety
- Frustration
- Stressful
- Useless
- Sucks
- Difficult
- Tedious
- Overwhelming
- Black hole
- Resume
- Internet

Read through the list of words again. What emotional response are *you* feeling? Negativity? Fear? Stress? All of these words are mostly negative, even scary and intimidating. Who would ever want to conduct a job search if these are the feelings we have about it? Nobody!

As for me, I felt just like Jennifer on Sundays when I worked for a large corporation and dreamed about getting a new job. Weekends always seemed like they should include another day. Sunday afternoons, I felt so overwhelmed about the upcoming workweek that it hindered my ability to enjoy the second half of my day. I always joked with my co-workers that I was going to wear a t-shirt under my blazer that said, "I Hate Mondays!"

Fast-forward to today, and oh how things have changed! I love Mondays! Each week, my entire Sundays are an enjoyable part of my weekend, free of overwhelm and anxiety. In fact, what I do feel at the end of every Sunday is excitement to get back to work Monday morning because I love what I do.

It is my hope that this book will prompt you to find work that you love to do, because I'll be the first to tell you — it feels awesome to do what you love!

When I think of job searching today, here are the words that come to mind:

- Exciting
- New
- Fresh
- Pay Raise
- Expanding Network
- Getting a Promotion
- Getting What I Want Out of My Career
- Expanding My Knowledge

Of course, the feelings I have about job searching are positive because this is what I do for a living — help people advance in their careers and find jobs they love. For the past fifteen years, I have put energy into helping other people have a positive job search experience. And you can have an enjoyable one, too!

Every day, we get to choose if we're going to see things in a positive or negative light. In this world, when some of the only things we can control are our thoughts and how we react to something, I challenge you to change your frame of mind. When you change your frame of mind to focus only on what is positive about a job search, it is very rewarding. The end result of finding a career you enjoy is incredible. You will be rewarded in numerous ways — earning more money, expanding your knowledge, and career advancement...allowing you to love your Mondays!

According to the Bureau of Labor Statistics, the average person held an average of 11.7 jobs from ages 18 to 48, with nearly half of these jobs held before age 25. That means between the ages of 25 to 48, we will change jobs roughly 6 times. Isn't this a sign that we all need help in finding the right job?[**]

If we only change jobs 6 times in 23 years, how can we have the knowledge to execute an effective job search?

[**] http://www.bls.gov/news.release/pdf/nlsoy.pdf

Introduction: You Can Stop Hating Mondays

Well, the answer is here…in your hands. This book is about the art of transforming your job search into a positive experience. This book will give you all the tools you need to execute an effective search when the need arises. You can use this book to find your next job and refer back to this book to sharpen your skills when it's time to look for the next one.

My goal is to pull back the curtain about what really goes into job searching, eliminating the negative and giving you specific **ACTION ITEMS** you can implement immediately.

Wouldn't it be terrific if YOU felt empowered to control where you were headed next in your career — the company, the position, and the timing — and eliminated those Sunday Blues? Wouldn't it be amazing if you could say, "I love Mondays!" and mean it?

The great news is that the tools to finding that empowerment are right here; all you have to do is make the time to read the book and complete the assignments.

 **ACTION ITEM:**

Carve out specific time in your calendar and dedicate it to your job search. Determine how much time (realistically) you have daily or weekly to devote to your job search. Once you've made this commitment, put it on your calendar and stick to it!

Write down these two things below:
1) The specific time you will dedicate 2) the intentional commitment you're making to chase your goal. *Example: I will dedicate 5pm — 5:30pm on Mondays, Wednesdays, Fridays, and 8am — 9am on Saturdays and Sundays to my job search because I deserve a better job.*

_____
_____
_____
_____
_____
_____
_____
_____
_____

CHAPTER 1

I WANT MORE
Clarify Your Job Needs and Desires

*"When you know what you want,
and you want it bad enough,
you'll find a way to get it."*

~ Jim Rohn ~

"JENNIFER, I'M PLEASED to meet you and very excited to help you find a new job. Let's start with WHY you're looking for a new job..." I smiled at the young lady in her early 30's sitting across from me, noticing that her countenance was dark and her shoulders slumped.

Wow, this lady looks beat up.

"Well..." she started, looking down at the ground. "I'm really looking for a change."

Wow, there must be something going on at her company that she isn't ready to share. After years of working with professionals searching for new jobs, I knew the signs like I knew the back of my hand.

"Okay, I understand that feeling. Tell me more."

She looked up at me, "I've been there for over six years and think it's time to make a change."

"And what is causing that desire for a change? You can be open with me. I'm here to help you," I reassured her.

"To be honest, Renee, I don't like the way they treat me or anyone else for that matter. The manager is never happy and always yelling. And I haven't gotten a raise in two years, even though I've been performing above my job responsibilities. It goes completely unnoticed by management."

"Oh my, that sounds awful. No one deserves to be treated like that. I truly appreciate you sharing that with me. They obviously don't see the value that you can offer their company. Let's work together to figure out the ideal situation for you. I'm going to go through a series of questions that will help us identify the right company and environment for you."

"That sounds wonderful!"

Her face brightened a little, and we went to work. Step one was uncovering all of the elements that were important to her in finding a new position.

Chapter 1: I Want More

"Jennifer, what gets you out of bed in the morning?"

"My alarm clock," she laughed.

I joined in the laughter and asked again.

"I love telling a story through data, helping the business achieve greater results through it," she said with crystal-clear confidence.

"What are the top three things that are most important to you in finding a new position?" I continued.

"Ummm, let me think. First, I want a company that will treat me with respect and as a professional. A company where I can continue to learn and advance my skills. And lastly, where I can be paid what I'm worth."

"All of those items are very reasonable, Jennifer. You'd be surprised how many companies offer those things that are most important to you."

She smiled, and a bit of hope began to emerge in her eyes.

Have you been in Jennifer's shoes before? I've heard a similar story from so many of my clients that I wouldn't doubt that some of this rings true for you as well.

Maybe you are working for a company that doesn't value you, and you have a desire for something greater. Perhaps you have outgrown your current company and feel you are ready for and deserve a promotion, but it never happens, leaving you at a dead-end.

Clearly you are seeking something different — something you are not getting out of your current job. When you begin your job search, you need to know exactly what you cannot tolerate at your current job and exactly what you are looking for in your next one.

Here are some of the most common reasons people change jobs:

- Gain more knowledge
- Work for a great leader
- Earn more money
- Enjoy a positive work environment
- Work for a company that aligns with your values
- Create a shorter commute
- Work in a position where you can soar with your strengths
- Adjust to life changes: marriage, divorce, birth/adoption of child, home purchase

ACTION ITEM:

Take a minute to visualize yourself in your ideal position, at your ideal company. What will that *look* like? What will that *feel* like? What do you want from your next position, company, manager, and yourself? It's like buying your dream house, or upgrading. Take time to consider what those things will mean to you. Visualize yourself in that ideal environment.

Now, create a list of all the things you do not like about your current job. Think in terms of money, culture, leadership, opportunity for career advancement, people you work with, etc. Be completely honest, as no one will read this but you. People often think it's all about the money, but they don't pay attention to the fact that they are being mistreated and undervalued. Keep in mind focusing just on compensation won't help you understand why you feel underpaid. By physically writing your feelings down on paper, you will help yourself move through this emotional decision with more courage and commitment.

What I dislike about my current job...
Ex: There is no flexibility. They clock the time I arrive and leave even though I'm salaried.

_____

_____

_____

What I desire and deserve...
Ex: I should be treated like a working professional and valued for the work I deliver.

_____

_____

_____

Now read through your list of what you wrote under "What I desire and deserve..." and rank them in order of importance to you, with #1 being the most important.

Write the 3 items that are most important to you here:

1. _____

_____

2. _____

_____

3. _____

_____

Your next job needs to consist of all 3 of these items. If it doesn't, you may end up in the same position you're in currently — looking for a new job.

Visit www.TalentQ.net/job-search for more tips.

CHAPTER 2

I'M OUTTA HERE
Write Your Resignation Letter

"The secret of change is to focus all of your energy, not on fighting the old, but on building the new."

~ Socrates ~

"OKAY, SO THE next thing I want you to do, Jennifer, is write your resignation letter to your current company."

"A what? Resignation letter? Really? I haven't even found a new job yet!" She was wide-eyed with worry.

"Yes, a resignation letter." I smiled. "Don't worry. I'm not asking you to resign today. I simply want you to go through the exercise of actually writing a resignation letter and then I'd like you to send it to me."

"Okay." She looked hesitantly at me, with big questions in her eyes.

"This is just a process that helps my clients anchor their decision that they are ready to leave their employer. This is critical to helping you emotionally detach from your current employer."

"That does make sense." She nodded in still-hesitant understanding.

"You have worked at your company for a few years and built strong relationships and friendships with many people there, I'm sure. You have integrated yourself into the culture. You know the routines of the company, there is a familiarity, and comfort of knowing those things, isn't there?"

"Yes, I do have lots of friends..." Jennifer looked down at her hands.

"When you write or type out your resignation letter, it's as if you've committed to the fact that you deserve better. While you are writing it, it may evoke emotions, or even create feelings of fear. If it does, review your top 3 things you must have in your next position. Then think about all the possibility that is out there for you!"

"Gosh, you're right, Renee. This isn't going to be easy emotionally, and this will probably help." She smiled as she left to work on her first assignment.

If you are reading this book, you've already decided to look for a new position, and you are clearly taking action and filling your brain with knowledge to enhance your job searching experience. And yet, the process can be emotional.

Accepting a new job ranks very high in the hierarchy of emotional decisions we make during our lifetime. It is the second most emotional decision you'll ever make, aside from marriage. The more you can prepare emotionally for this significant change, the better.

You will need to be fully emotionally prepared to ignite your job search and put all of your energy behind it.

You are probably thinking as Jennifer did, *"Write my resignation letter? Isn't that the last step when I find a new job?"*

I'm clearly here to turn your world upside-down.

Writing your resignation letter is one of the first steps in your job search because if you don't psychologically and emotionally begin to separate yourself from your employer, you will question if you should stay…even if you find a job that is exactly what you want.

You'll think to yourself: *"Maybe tomorrow will get better," "Maybe my company will value me eventually," "Maybe my review will be better this year and I will be promoted," "Maybe I will receive a pay raise…"*

"Maybe, maybe, maybe..." basically talking yourself into staying at the company and in the position you are in. And yet, your employer will not change. Your employer will not value you more. That ship has sailed. It's time to find one that will meet all of your needs and desires.

I know you have built relationships with your co-workers and have people you consider friends at work. You have daily routines that are comfortable. You know the job well and understand the company. You know who to go to when you need things. You have immersed yourself into the company culture. These are all strong emotional strings that make you feel attached to your employer.

Writing your resignation letter will feel uncomfortable at first, and it will also feel incredibly liberating to commit yourself to finding a much better opportunity. Cut those emotional strings tying you to the company in preparation for your new position and employer.

# ACTION ITEM:

Write your resignation letter and keep it somewhere safe. Once you land the perfect job, you'll be ready to use it!

I've included a sample resignation letter, with all of the fundamental elements (date, statement of resignation, gratitude, end date, and your signature). It should be customized so that it feels authentic to you and has the correct information in it.

YOUR NAME
ADDRESS
CITY, STATE ZIP
PHONE NUMBER

DATE

RECIPIENT NAME
TITLE
COMPANY ADDRESS
CITY, STATE ZIP

Dear NAME,

Please accept this letter as my formal resignation from my position as <TITLE>. My last day of employment at <COMPANY NAME> will be <DATE>.

I would like to express my gratitude for the wonderful opportunities I have been given at

<COMPANY NAME> for professional growth and development. I have learned so much and greatly enjoyed working with such a supportive and dynamic team.

While I am excited by the new opportunities that I will be pursuing, I will always remember my time at <COMPANY NAME> with great fondness. Please do not hesitate to contact me if you need any further information after I leave. I wish you and the company success in the future.

Best regards,
(sign your name)
YOUR NAME

www.TalentQ.net/job-search for more tips.

Chapter 2: I'm Outta Here

When you have written a resignation letter, you have made the decision to leave your employer and are ready to transfer your loyalty to a new one. Make that commitment to yourself. You deserve better. Life is too short to spend one-third of your life in a job that doesn't fulfill you.

CHAPTER 3

I'M LOOKING GOOD

Create a Killer Resume and LinkedIn Profile

"Change before you have to."
~ Jack Welch ~

JENNIFER SAT ACROSS from me, frustrated as she looked down at her resume. "I know, I don't like resumes either," I offered, trying to lighten the mood.

She looked up at me in surprise and I continued, "Resumes are tough because you have to capture your career and accomplishments, as well as your strengths and character, on one sheet of paper. It is absurd, I know. When you look at your professional career, there is A LOT involved, so much work you have accomplished, years of knowledge and experience. There is much more to you, Jennifer, than words on a page of paper. If we work together, we can go through this process of refining all of that into one or two pages. Let's break it down one element at a time."

Holding her pen and notebook, she nodded in readiness.

"Let's start at the top. Objectives are not needed. If you've applied to a particular job, that is your intent — you would like to be considered for the job you applied for. Objectives are just taking up valuable space on your paper that can be used for something else."

"I always wondered why you stated the job you were looking for on your resume. I mean, I'm obviously interested if I applied." Her raised eyebrow made me laugh at the absurdity with her.

"A better option is a Summary — a few sentences of key selling points about you and your background. It is a brief description of you, so the person reading your resume will read it entirely. It is the first thing they will read about you."

"That makes sense." Her face was beginning to brighten a little.

"Jennifer, think about a few things that you are most known for in your position. It could be superior customer service, the ability to explain technical information to non-technical people, or passion for data."

"Oh! I'm really good at explaining technical information to non-technical folks." She immediately sat up straighter in her chair, displaying her confidence.

"Okay, that's a good start."

"And I'm passionate about data!" she exclaimed.

"Great! So we could start your summary with *'Passionate individual who drives business results through data. Highly skilled at communicating technical information to non- technical individuals.'"*

"That sounds perfect!" she nearly squealed.

"The next step is making sure your Summary connects to the job for which you are applying. Depending on the position, I'm assuming in most roles, you will be collaborating with other teams, perhaps project teams, and the business, etc.?"

"Yes, I really enjoy that part."

"Okay, we will want to add something like, *'Collaborative team player who builds strong relationships.'"*

"I love it!" Her smile was growing.

We both looked at what we came up with for Jennifer's summary:

Passionate individual who drives business results through data. Highly skilled at communicating technical information to non-technical individuals. Collaborative team player who builds strong relationships.

Visit www.TalentQ.net/job-search for more tips.

Did you know that recruiters only look at the top one-third of the first page of your resume before they decide if they will contact you for a position or politely put your resume in the recycle bin? On average, a recruiter only spends 6 seconds reviewing a resume to determine whether you are a fit for the open position.

There was a study done by TheLadders, which was based on data from an eye-tracking study of thirty professional recruiters who were monitored over a ten-week period as they evaluated resumes and candidate profile reviews. Here's a visual demonstration of what they found:

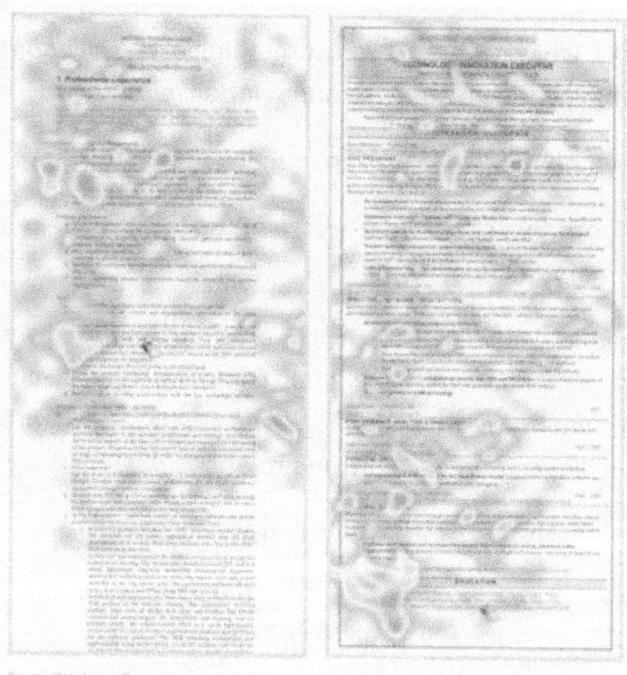

Source: Keeping an Eye on Recruiter Behavior, TheLadders, 2014

As you can see, the resume on the left doesn't start with a Summary, and isn't as formatted as the one on the right, and the recruiter looked at it briefly. The resume on the right was evaluated entirely.

That's why it's so important to have a powerful Summary at the top of your resume. Hook 'em right away! Make them excited to keep reading.

Examples of Summaries

Accomplished recruiter with 15+ years of professional experience in full-cycle recruiting. Exceeds goals by passionately embracing business needs with strategy and creative sourcing methods to identify top talent. Savvy business partner who builds strong relationships with internal and external clients.

Strategic business leader with proven track record of implementing consumer-based strategies to drive business impact, combined with a passion for developing teams. A history of taking strategic risks to lean into meaningful opportunities through product launches, resource investment, and partnerships.

Ambitious and dedicated engineer with a proven track record of developing innovative solutions and refining workflows. Prioritizes work to align with key business strategies. Exceptional interpersonal skills and genuine commitment to quality and customer satisfaction.

Accomplished and experienced management professional with a record of achievement in driving improvement in sales, operations planning, supply chain cost management, and customer service. An expert in building and fostering solid relationships with internal and external customers. Noted for consistently elevating sales and profitability through the adoption of customer-centric sales approaches that ensure exceptional quality in products and services.

Visit www.TalentQ.net/job-search for more tips.

# ACTION ITEM:

Write your Summary.

Think about the key selling points about your background. Do some brainstorming here: Next, what are you most known for in your position? Write those items here:

_____
_____
_____
_____
_____
_____

What characteristics are needed in the job you are applying for or the job you want to get? Jot them down here.

_____
_____
_____
_____
_____
_____

Next, go back and look at all of the statements you wrote down. Circle the ones you like the best and weave them together to come up with your summary. Keep in mind these sentences should be key selling points about your background and hook the reader into reading your entire resume. If you need help with descriptive adjectives, take a look at the list below and use the words you like throughout the whole process of resume writing.

_____

_____

_____

_____

_____

_____

Examples of Powerful Words

Able	Delegated	Gained
Accomplished	Deliver	Gathered
Achievement	Dependable	Gave
Action	Design	Generated
Active	Determined	Headed
Adaptable	Develop	Hosted
Advanced	Devoted	Identified
Agile	Disciplined	Implemented
Ambitious	Distinguished	Improved
Analysis	Diversified	Improvised
Analytical	Dynamic	Influenced
Assist	Earned	Innovative
Attentive	Efficient	Launched
Collaborative	Encourage	Lobbied
Committed	Energetic	Maintained
Conduct	Enhance	Managed
Conducted	Enthusiastic	Marketed
Conscientious	Evaluate	Maximized
Consult	Examine	Mediated
Contributed	Extensive	Methodical
Coordinated	Facilitate	Modernized
Creative	Flexible	Motivated
Customer-focused	Forecasted	Negotiated
Customer-centric	Formulate	Objective
Defined	Fulfilled	Observed

Obtained	Ranked	Strengthened
Operated	Received	Structured
Optimistic	Recommended	Suggested
Organized	Redesigned	Superseded
Originated	Reengineered	Supervised
Overhauled	Reliable	Systematic
Oversaw	Reorganized	Takes initiative
Participated	Represented	Targeted
Performed	Resilient	Taught
Personable	Resourceful	Tenacious
Pioneered	Respectful	Tested
Planned	Restructured	Trained
Positive	Revised	Transcended
Prepared	Safeguarded	Unified
Presented	Savvy	Upgraded
Proactive	Secured	Utilized
Productive	Selected	Validated
Promoted	Self-starter	Valued
Provided	Spearheaded	Versatile
Published	Specified	Wrote
Pursued	Standardized	
Quantified	Strategic	

Chapter 3: I'm Looking Good

Jennifer was so excited about her Summary, she asked, "What's next? What else has to go on this thing?"

"Well, there is the obvious piece of your Contact Information. I know it seems obvious, but you'd be surprised. I have people send me resumes with just their name — no email, no phone number, no city. But you need all of these. And your name needs to be the biggest words on the page at the top. In looking at your resume, Jennifer, your Contact Information looks fine."

"Well that part was easy. I already had it right!"

"Next is Education. Since you have more than 5 years of experience, you can decide where to put your Education. It could go after your Summary or after your Professional Experience. That is up to you. For new college grads, I recommend putting the Education after their Summary, as most do not have extensive work experience upon graduation. New college graduates rely heavily on their Education to help them land their first career after graduation. You, on the other hand, have 8 years of work experience so you can decide. With the Education section, you need to list the name of the college you attended, city and state (if it is not in the title of the college), graduation year, any honors and, if your GPA was above a 3.0, feel free to list it."

I looked up to see her eyebrows scrunch into a question I hear a lot, "Why above 3.0 GPA?"

"A lot of companies have GPA parameters for new college graduates so if your GPA was below a 3.0, there is no need to list it. GPA is completely optional. I personally don't think it should be listed, as it's another component that can pigeon-hole you during resume evaluation. If you were on the Dean's List or graduated with honors, that is more powerful than a good GPA. Plus, the more work experience you have and the further you get away from your graduation, the less important it is."

"That makes sense." Jennifer's shoulders had finally relaxed, and it seemed easier for her to follow along with me.

"Now to the best part of the resume: Professional Experience. You did a great job, Jennifer, listing the company, the location, the dates you were employed there, and your titles. Way to go!"

"Thanks, Renee!"

"Let's go through each bullet under each position, line-by-line. Here is a sheet of powerful descriptive words you can refer to while writing your resume." I handed her a list of words. "What you are trying to convey in this area are details about what you specifically did, so that anyone reading it can understand the work you performed. Make sense?"

"Yes, but at our company, we had so many acronyms." She clearly understood that acronyms are often culture-

or industry-specific and can confuse more than help if not explained.

"Oh, I'm sure! I remember working in Corporate America — there were acronyms for everything! Make sure you avoid the use of acronyms, and write what it stands for instead. As you list out your job duties, what you want to do is list the most important items or items highest in scope at the top, then continue in decreasing order of importance as you go down the page. You want to put as much data as possible into these statements of job duties. If you have any concerns about divulging confidential information, then instead of dollar amounts, you can describe data in terms of percentages. For example, 'increased revenue by 21% year-over-year.' Don't limit yourself in thinking data is only dollar amounts. Data can be days, time, percentages, ratios, etc."

"Interesting, I never thought to put more data on my resume, even though that's my passion," Jennifer smirked at the irony.

I smiled back, "Indeed! So let's go through line-by-line and I'll help you jazz the statements up and make them more clear to an outsider who doesn't work for your company. As you worked for the same company for 3 years and were promoted, you don't need to list out the company name again. We can just put your different titles under the company and put the dates next to it in parenthesis to show the upward progression."

"Awesome! That way, we are saving space too."

"Exactly!"

Contact Information

This is the first item on your resume, and it should include your name, address OR city and state at a minimum, one phone number, and one email address. Your name should be the largest words on the page. It is optional to list a link to your LinkedIn profile or Twitter handle. If you have suspect Tweets or anything that could cause someone to question your character, I would not list it. If your job involves social media, list it to showcase your experience. Below is an example of how you can format your Contact Information.

Jennifer A. Hanson
1234 Awesome St, Minneapolis, MN 55402 • 612-123-1234 • jenniferhanson@email.com

SUMMARY
Passionate individual who drives business results through data. Highly skilled at communicating technical information to non-technical individuals. Collaborative team player who builds strong relationships.

Education

Education can be placed in one of two areas. If you are a recent college graduate, put the Education after the Summary.

If it has been a while since you graduated and you have over 7 years of experience, put the Education after Professional Experience. Essentially if you have working experience, you can decide where to put the Education on your resume; the longer you have been in the workforce, the less your Education matters and the more your working experience does.

In the Education section, list the institution you attended, what city and state it was in. If the state is in the name of the school, there is no need for redundancy. Include the degree you received and the year you graduated. If your GPA was above 3.0, feel free to include it. If it was below a 3.0, omit it. Also, if you have over 20+ years of experience, the year you graduated is optional. Even though in the US, we cannot discriminate on age, some choose not to list their year of graduation in an effort to keep them from figuring out their age.

Jennifer A. Hanson
1234 Awesome St, Minneapolis, MN 55402 • 612-123-1234 • jenniferhanson@email.com

SUMMARY
Passionate individual who drives business results through data. Highly skilled at communicating technical information to non-technical individuals. Collaborative team player who builds strong relationships.

PROFESSIONAL EXPERIENCE
North State Inc, Minneapolis, MN   March 2008 – Present
Sr. Business Intelligence Analyst (Feb 2013 to Present)
- Create, Business Intelligence solutions through dashboard style reporting to the workspace and mobile devices.
- Support over 400 Desktop Users utilizing Cognos Business Intelligence, and Tableau Visualization
- Generate self-service climate via multi-dimensional cube analysis to foster a single source of truth.
- Gather business requirements from each department to generate the reports they need.
- Design, create and maintain interactive dashboards to enable end users to generate their own ad-hoc queries
- Enhance existing queries to pull more accurate and relevant data for analysis.
- Collaborate with the data warehouse team to optimize performance in Business Intelligence tools using an agile approach.
- Administration of systems, comprised of installation, configuration, data quality, metadata modeling, Oracle SQL, security and solution development

Data Analyst (May 2010 to Feb 2013)
- Design, maintain and communicate client proposals and worksheets.
- Manage and monitor orders through manufacturing, shipping, receiving, and shipments to customers.
- Analyze sales orders to ensure data accuracy.
- Analyze and transform raw data into user-friendly reports and dashboards.
- Develop end-to-end automated reporting solutions for recurring reporting needs.
- Create sales reports to generate promotion reimbursement to clients.

Data Specialist (March 2008 to May 2010)
- Track new accounts from start to finish in system.
- Manage all sales commission activity for sales representatives based on territory, corporate objectives and present to VP of Sales for approval and payout.
- Enter sales commission data into dashboard for leadership team review.
- Point of contact for any questions regarding commission activity.

EDUCATION
University of Minnesota, Minneapolis, MN   Bachelors of Science in Computer Science   2008
Dean's List, Honors Program

AWARDS
- CIO Award, May 2014

SPECIALIZED TRAINING
- Toastmasters International
- Fluent in French

COMMUNITY INVOLEMENT
- Treasurer, Tall Tree Homeowner Association, 2015 to present
- Big Sister at Big Brothers Big Sisters of Minnesota 2008 - Present

Chapter 3: I'm Looking Good

"Okay, Jennifer, now that we have your Education and Professional Experience written out, let's look at the last few elements of your resume. And let's start with Awards... have you been presented with any awards?"

"Oh yes, I won an award for a project I was on." Her eyes sparkled with pride.

"Congratulations! Let's list that on here. When did you receive that award?"

"I just received it two months ago."

"Fantastic! Any others?"

"I won 'most animated' at a team-building event!" She laughed out loud.

"That's fun and great, but we'll keep that one off the resume." I laughed with her.

"Okay, that's the only one then."

"Great. Next is Certifications. What Certifications do you hold?" I started.

"Ummm, I don't have any," she responded flatly.

"That's just fine. Do you have any Specialized Training?" I continued.

"What do you mean by that?" She started to look concerned.

"For example, I took a course called Power Talk when I was employed by a large corporation that helped us enhance our public speaking ability."

"No, I don't have anything like that. We did read Strengths Finder and had a team exercise around it," she offered.

"You could list that there. Have you ever been in Toastmasters?" I asked.

"Yes, I'm actually a member now."

"Awesome! Do you volunteer anywhere?" I coaxed.

"Yes, I love volunteering. I'm a Big Sister in the Big Brother Big Sisters program." Again, her posture straightened and her smile returned.

"Dynamite! Volunteering is so fulfilling! Good for you! Let's add that under community involvement. Anything else?" I felt like maybe there was still something we were missing.

"What about the fact I'm fluent in French?" she questioned.

"Oh cool! We can put that on there too! We only list languages you are fluent in; and if it were a job requirement to speak French, you would definitely want to list it. For example, I'm fluent in American Sign Language because

Chapter 3: I'm Looking Good

my mom is Deaf, but I do not list it on my resume. I do have it listed on my LinkedIn profile though."

"I see..." she responded. "You mentioned LinkedIn, that reminds me...should I update my profile there too?"

"Most definitely! That part will be a piece of cake now that your resume is complete!" I assured her.

"Whew!" Relief washed over both of us as we looked at her powerful new resume.

I Hate Mondays

Jennifer A. Hanson

1234 Awesome St, Minneapolis, MN 55402
612-123-1234 • jenniferhanson@email.com

SUMMARY

Passionate individual who drives business results through data. Highly skilled at communicating technical information to non-technical individuals. Collaborative team player who builds strong relationships.

PROFESSIONAL EXPERIENCE

North State Inc, Minneapolis, MN   March 2008 – Present

Sr. Business Intelligence Analyst (Feb 2013 – Present)
- Create, Business Intelligence solutions through dashboard style reporting to the workspace and mobile devices
- Support over 400 Desktop Users utilizing Cognos Business Intelligence, and Tableau Visualizations
- Generate self-service climate via multi-dimensional cube analysis to foster a single source of truth
- Gather business requirements from each department to generate the reports they need
- Design, create and maintain interactive dashboards to enable end users to generate their own ad-hoc queries
- Enhance existing queries to pull more accurate and relevant data for analysis
- Collaborate with the data warehouse team to optimize performance in Business Intelligence tools using an agile approach
- Administration of systems, comprised of installation, configuration, data quality, metadata modeling, Oracle SQL, security and solution development

Data Analyst (May 2010 – Feb 2013)
- Design, maintain and communicate client proposals and worksheets
- Manage and monitor orders through manufacturing, shipping, receiving, and shipments to customers
- Audit sales orders to ensure data accuracy
- Analyze and transform raw data into user-friendly reports and dashboards
- Develop end-to-end automated reporting solutions for recurring reporting needs
- Create sales reports to generate promotion reimbursement to clients

Data Specialist (March 2008 – May 2010)
- Track new accounts from start to finish in system
- Manage all sales commission activity for sales representatives based on territory, corporate objectives and present to VP of Sales for approval and payout
- Enter sales commission data into dashboard for leadership team review
- Point of contact for any questions regarding commission activity

EDUCATION

University of Minnesota, Minneapolis, MN
Bachelors of Science in Computer Science   2008
Dean's List, Honors Program

AWARDS

- CIO Award, May 2014

SPECIALIZED TRAINING

- Toastmasters International
- Fluent in French

COMMUNITY INVOLVEMENT

- Treasurer, Tall Tree Homeowner Association, 2015 to present
- Big Sister at Big Brothers Big Sisters of Minnesota 2008 — Present

Optional Sections

All of these sections on your resume are completely optional. You may be a new college graduate and still need to acquire experience in these areas. If you have them, make sure you choose the ones best suited to the position you're applying for.

- Awards
- Certifications
- Specialized Training
- Community Involvement
- Languages

Organization of Your Resume

Now that you have all of the elements of your resume written, organize them according to your particular amount of experience. See instructions below.

If you're a recent college grad, use this order:

- Contact Information
- Summary
- Education
- Professional Experience, which includes internships
- Awards, Certifications, Specialized Training, and Community Involvement (which can go in any order you wish)

If you have more than 7 years of professional experience, use this order:

- Contact Information
- Summary
- Professional Experience
- Education
- Awards, Certifications, Specialized Training, and Volunteer Experience (which can go in any order you wish)

Chapter 3: I'm Looking Good

 **ACTION ITEM:**

It's time to work on all of these elements of your resume and put them together. Ready. Set. Go.

Key Resume Tips
Ensure your resume is visually appealing by reviewing it, and even having someone else review it, for the following items:

- Always write in 3rd person. Never use "I" or "me".
- Streamline all of the formatting.
- Use the same font for all of the text.
- Align the margins on both sides.
- Make sure your bullet points are aligned.
- Make sure the spacing of each section is the same.
- Make sure indents are the same down the entire page.
- Either use periods in your whole resume or do not use any periods.
- Do a thorough grammar check.
- Perform a spellcheck.
- Omit acronyms and write out the words on your resume.
- Use descriptive adjectives to describe the work you have performed.
- Use data to enhance your statements.

I Hate Mondays

What NOT to do in a resume:

Renee J. Frey
765, New City, MN 55402 • 612-345-6789 • myemail@email.com •

SUMMARY
Accomplished recruiter with 14+ years of professional experience in full-cycle recruiting. Exceeds goals by passionately embracing business needs with strategy and creative sourcing methods to identify top talent. Savvy business partner who builds strong relationships with internal and external clients.

PROFESSIONAL EXPERIENCE
TalentQ, Inc., Hudson, WI   Mar 2015 – Present
Founder/President
Recruiting firm specializing in contract and direct hire placement of exceptional talent nationwide
- Strategically prospect for companies and hiring managers who have hiring needs to grow our client base
- Create and present TalentQ's business overview to obtain new business
- Negotiate terms and conditions of contracts.
- Conduct thorough intake meeting with hiring leaders to uncover ideal candidate's qualifications.
- Create strategic recruiting plans to identify candidates who meet the requirements of our clients
- Creatively source high caliber candidates through various methods which include cold-calling, networking, internet resources, social media, associations, trade shows, conferences, meet ups and referrals
- Influence hiring decisions candidates by assessing talent through behavioral based interviews, facilitating selection decisions with clients.
- Champion social media recruitment, recruiting best practices, diversity recruitment, share industry trends
- Accountable for key metrics including: interview-to-offer, offer-to-accept, diversity rate, days-to-fill, and expense management

Target Corporation, Minneapolis, MN   Dec 2007 – Mar 2015
Executive Recruiter (June 2012 to present)
Successfully hired candidates for various Divisions: Property Development, Distribution, Stores, Finance, Target.com and Technology
- SWAT Talent Acquisition team is a flexible recruiting team that supports all of Target's divisions nationwide, solving enterprise wide talent needs through recruitment, consultation & development
- Strategically align recruitment needs to business objectives while considering cost per hire
- Develop strategic recruiting plans to ensure diverse talent pipeline through effective recruiting methods
- Creatively source high caliber candidates through various methods which include cold-calling, networking, internet resources, social media, associations, trade shows, conferences, meet ups and employee referrals
- Influence hiring decisions for internal and external candidates by assessing talent through behavioral based interviews, facilitating selection decisions with internal clients: manager to SVP level
- Primary contact for hiring manager and HR generalist to proactively manage staffing needs
- Champion social media recruitment, recruiting best practices, diversity recruitment, share industry trends
- Accountable for key metrics including: interview-to-offer, offer-to-accept, diversity rate, days-to-fill, and expense management
- Lead, created, and presented recruiter acumen training to 150 recruiters focused on partner influence
- On-board, train, develop, and mentor other recruiters and sourcers
- Facilitate Interview Certification training for hiring managers
- Attend conferences such as Grace Hopper, NBMBAA, NSHMBA as a brand ambassador to educate and attract top talent to Target

Senior Recruiter – Merchandising, Sourcing and Marketing Divisions (May 2010 – June 2012)
Successfully hired candidates for the following positions: Buyers, Product Managers, Packaging Specialists/Senior, Marketing Specialists/Managers, Packaging Engineers/Senior/Managers Quality Assurance Analysts, Quality Assurance Engineers/Senior/Managers, Social Compliance & Sustainability Managers, Systems Analysts, Product Safety Recall Analysts, Operations Process Analysts, Operations Experts
- Exceeded Buyer hiring goal by 305% over results in 2010
- Developed holistic recruitment strategy, structure, and media plan to hire Buyers and Product Managers
- Created Talent Acquisition Partnership Strategy for internal clients to promote clarity with recruitment

"Jennifer, before we move on to your LinkedIn profile, I would like you to Google your name and see what comes up." I was feeling very enthusiastic about this young woman's future.

"Okay...?" Her statement was more of a question.

"There are some employers that Google the people who apply to their company to check them out and see what type of online presence they have. You want to make sure every social media channel you are a part of portrays you in a professional and decent manner."

"Those are great tips. I had no idea employers actually did that."

Employers frequently Google their applicants to learn more about them. In order to make sure they are thrilled by what they see, you can set your privacy settings on any channel as well as audit your profiles with the major search engines so you know what others can see if you Google your name. The goal is to maintain a professional online presence. You want to be positive, authentic, and engaging.

 **ACTION ITEM:**

Google your name and evaluate what comes up. Remember you want to have a professional presence. If you question any of the posts or pictures you have, that probably means you should delete them or make them so only you can view them. Every social media channel that you have a profile on needs to be filtered.

Here is a list of some of the most popular social media channels you may have a presence on: LinkedIn, Facebook, Twitter, Instagram, YouTube, Pinterest, and Snapchat.

"Jennifer, you have a great professional online presence, so there is nothing to worry about there. Let's move on to LinkedIn!"

"Gosh, you really love this stuff, don't you?" she asked.

"I sure do! You ready?" I wanted to make sure she didn't need a break.

"Yes, I am!" Her excitement suddenly matched mine.

"The first thing we need to do is turn off the notifications that LinkedIn sends out to all of your connections when you change anything on your page."

"Oh my! I had no idea they did that." She quickly turned off the notifications from her laptop.

"Yep, most users are not aware of this. Go to your LinkedIn profile. You will see a section on the right hand side that says 'Notify your network.' Click on the word 'Yes' to turn it off. However, we will want to turn this on when you upload your photo. A little secret of mine — when you upload your photo, you get the most views on your page, which is perfect if you're looking for a new position."

"Awesome!" she exclaimed.

"Now that you have a killer resume, LinkedIn is a piece of cake. On your LinkedIn page, click Profile at the top of your homepage. Move your cursor over the down arrow next to 'View Profile As' button and select 'Import Resume.' Click 'Choose File' or 'Browse' to locate your resume on your computer and click 'Upload Resume.' Got it?"

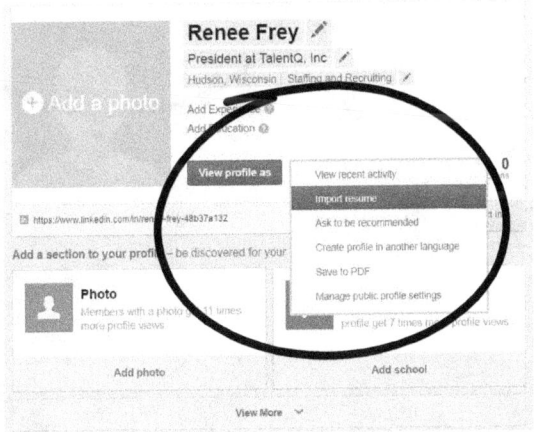

"Yes, I got it. That's slick!" The techy in her obviously loved how streamlined and easy this actually was.

"Sure is! Now you can modify and move the areas in your LinkedIn profile to where you want them. If you want, you can add more to your Summary on LinkedIn. And it's okay to use the word 'I' on LinkedIn in the Summary. Another area you will want to put details in is under your name. If you hover your cursor over the top section, you will see little gray pencils. You can click and edit any of those. The headline is right under your name and that is what people will see first, so keep it professional and make it stand out."

As I coached her through the process, she made the changes quickly.

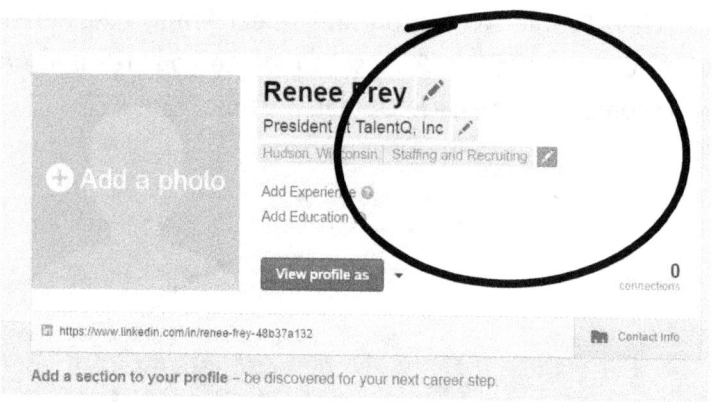

Chapter 3: I'm Looking Good

"I notice that you don't have any recommendations on LinkedIn. We need to get you some. Who could you ask to make a recommendation on your behalf?"

"I could ask my peer, John, who won the award with me?" she asked.

"Excellent idea! Reach out to him and ask if he can complete a recommendation for you. The more you have, the better. What about people you volunteer with at Big Brothers Big Sisters? You can ask them too."

"I will," she said, making a note on the notepad on the desk between us.

"The Skills and Endorsements is an area you'll want to select some items that you have. Then LinkedIn sends questions to your connections, asking if you know about these things. If people agree they click 'Yes' and it goes on your profile. If you achieve over 99+, that's the max number it will say. Next to the skills listing are the photos of the people who have endorsed you. You can request people to endorse you as well."

"Cool!"

"Jennifer, let's change the notification setting back to ON to publish an update to your network about your profile changes, then upload your photo, sound good?"

"Yes!" She clicked it to ON and smiled. "That was easy!"

Key LinkedIn Tips

LinkedIn will walk you through setting up your account. Follow all the prompts and select the information or use the "skip" button. You can always go back to the items you skipped. Any edit you make on your LinkedIn page is defaulted to "Notify Your Network," so if you are making significant changes to your LinkedIn, people will be notified at every change you make. My suggestion is turning off the notifications while you make the updates. It is highlighted below where to find that option. When you have made all of your changes, do not forget to turn this button back on.

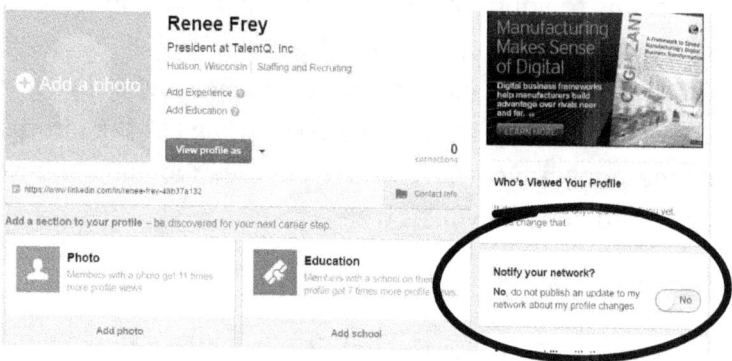

Make sure you use a professional photo. Do not crop your spouse out of your wedding photo and use that. If you want a new job, you want to have a professional-looking photo. If you do not have a nice headshot of yourself, you can get one from a photographer for a small investment. It will be worth it. If a hiring leader looks you up on LinkedIn, your photo will be their first impression of you.

A tip to remember: When changes are made to a profile picture, that is when people receive the most views. So if your intent is to obtain a new job, I suggest attracting as much attention to your LinkedIn profile as possible. Make sure the "Notify Your Network" button is green and turned to Yes, but only after your profile is in tip-top shape.

Please keep in mind LinkedIn is constantly changing the interface and functionality.

> Visit www.TalentQ.net/job-search for more tips.

CHAPTER 4

I'M ON THE HUNT
Leverage Your Network

*"Alone we can do so little;
together we can do so much."*
~ Helen Keller ~

"JENNIFER, HAVE YOU ever heard the saying, 'It's all about who you know'?" I relaxed back into my chair.

"Oh most definitely!" She nodded.

"Believe it or not, who you know is the best way for you to find a new job."

"Really?"

"Absolutely! Before starting my own company, I worked for five different companies. Aside from the first job I received out of college, which I landed from a job fair I attended, the other four were all through a connection with someone I knew. Either I reached out to them to inquire about opportunities at their companies or they called to recruit me because of our connection. When someone knows you and has worked with or for you in the past, they know your character, tendencies, and how you performed in your job previously. Knowing all of those components, they can speak to and share them with their current leadership team. A connection like this provides the company a higher comfort level, a familiarity, that they don't have with someone they do not know and only met during the interview process."

"That makes sense."

"These connections make hiring people less risky and more comfortable. Think about it this way: Past performance can predict future performance. Employee referrals continue to lead as the best source to find candidates because the quality of the candidate is higher, and retention is higher. Birds of a feather flock together." I smiled. "You would be surprised at how many people will want to help you."

"Tell me more." Jennifer leaned back comfortably in her chair.

"It is human nature to want to help others, and the people you know will want to help introduce you to people they know or, better yet, submit you as a referral for a position at the company they work for. Often employees are incentivized by referring candidates they think will be great for their company."

"We have an employee referral program at our company. We get $500 for referring people we hire," Jennifer affirmed enthusiastically.

"See, it is tremendously valued by companies. You should tell everyone you know you are looking for a new position or are open to new opportunities... Well, everyone except your current employer of course."

"Okay, how would I go about doing that? I haven't been a big networker."

"Numerous ways. You can mention it in any casual conversation, send out a crafted email to your network, or..." I paused. "First, let's brainstorm a little and make a list of people that may be able to help you. This could be anyone or even an acquaintance, or a friend of a friend. Jennifer, think about previous managers, co-workers, previous co-workers, peers, neighbors, fellow volunteers, church members, fellow alumni, networking groups, meet ups, friends on Facebook, connections on other social media platforms who work at the companies that interest you. Start making a list of them."

"It may take some time to compile this list," she said, as she started to jot down her list of people to consider.

"No problem. Once you have the list written down or typed up, go through it and highlight those you know best or those who work at companies you admire most. Reach out to them first. Let them know you are looking for a new opportunity and ask if they can refer you. Better yet, I would go to the company's website and search their careers portal to see if there are any opportunities that match your background. If there are, reference the position when you reach out and ask them to submit you as a referral. Also, ask who the position reports to so you can follow up."

"Great! I'm actually really excited to do this!"

ACTION ITEM:

Make a list of your network. Determine a ranking system of the people you know and highlight the people on the list who are the most influential, in leadership positions, or those who work at companies for which you want to work. Put these people at the top of the list and reach out to them first. If you have numerous connections on LinkedIn, you can export your contacts into a spreadsheet for easy sorting. (Go to Google for instructions on how to export your LinkedIn contacts.)

After you have done this, make a commitment to always be networking. This will help you in the future if you are in this situation again. Make sure you are networking, not only when you are looking for a new job but even when you have a job you love. It is extremely beneficial and will pay off.

Rekindling your network can feel like climbing Mount Everest. Take the first step, keep at it, and you will be surprised at what unfolds. Plus it will be so fun hearing what is new with these individuals. They will be thrilled to hear from you!

Ideas for Networking
There are hundreds of ways to network with others. You could attend networking events, conferences, trade shows, meet ups, church groups etc.

Set a goal prior to arriving to the event. A simple goal may be to talk to one person you do not know and connect with them. You may want to set a bigger goal for how many new people you want to meet at the event and reward yourself for achieving it with something that will motivate you to do it. If you are naturally outgoing, this may not be an issue for you. On the flip side, if you are introverted, the thought of networking may create some anxiety for you. Rest assured, your efforts will be worth it. Just take the first step.

Some reward ideas I've found helpful include:

- ❏ Treat yourself to a relaxing night
- ❏ Go to a movie

- ❑ Visit a new place and enjoy the adventure
- ❑ Take some time to create something
- ❑ Enjoy a coffee break
- ❑ Buy a new item for your wardrobe
- ❑ Get a massage
- ❑ Buy a new book

At the networking event, be unforgettable. Wear bright-colored pants, a bold red to boost your confidence. Perhaps you don't feel you can pull off red pants, but wear something striking that will stand out from the crowd — a red tie, a bold necklace. Get creative. Skip gray and black. Dress one step above the expected dress code. What this means is that if you expect people to be wearing business casual at the event, wear a suit or a dress. In a crowd, you need to think of little ways to stand out so you are memorable.

Have a killer smile, as this is the best accessory. Smiling acts like a magnet for positivity. When you smile, you look approachable and welcoming.

If you've heard the phrase "fake it until you make it," that's what it's all about. If you are uncomfortable, just smile, and one day you will feel comfortable. Make others feel good, compliment each person you meet about something with their appearance and be genuine about it. If this is too far out of your comfort zone, have a firm handshake and look people in the eye. Don't just exchange business cards. Connect with others. Ask thoughtful questions.

Here are some examples:

- ❑ What is the best book you've read recently? Why did you enjoy it?
- ❑ How can I add value or help you achieve your goals?
- ❑ What was your favorite travel destination?
- ❑ What's on your bucket list?
- ❑ Where did you grow up?
- ❑ What is your position/title?
- ❑ What are your responsibilities?
- ❑ Why does your field of work interest you and how did you get started?
- ❑ How did you get your job? What experiences have led you to this career/occupation?
- ❑ What skills are most important for you to do your job well? Do any of your personal traits help you?
- ❑ How did your college experience prepare you for your current role?

- ❑ What kinds of experience would you suggest for someone wanting to enter the same field as you?
- ❑ What types of changes have you seen lately within your profession?
- ❑ What are some pressures, problems, or challenges that someone entering into this career may face?
- ❑ What would you tell someone who wants to learn more about your field?

Memorize a few of your favorites from the list or come up with your own.

These questions go beyond asking what the person thought about the weather today, and day-to-day chitchat, and allow you to connect with them, showing you have an interest in them. These types of questions will impress them, showing you want to learn more about them, not get something from them. They will help you stand out and make you memorable.

Networking is a powerful tool that each and every person can benefit from. It is the single best way to find your next job.

You may be thinking, "I don't want to bother people with my job search." Come on! People who love their jobs and companies they work for want to help you feel the same.

They also want the broader network of helping the person that is lucky enough to hire you...everyone is going to benefit, not just you.

I recommend networking frequently and often. NEVER EVER STOP. Some company cultures can be very strong where they give you tunnel vision on focusing all your efforts on networking internally. However, you must look at the company you work for as a temporary gig — always have a 10,000 foot view approach, knowing that at some point, you're likely going to want to move on. You must continue to foster a good network of people, as chances are you will not be retiring with the company you work for today.

Tips if you have anxiety meeting others:

- ❑ Wear what makes you feel the most confident.
- ❑ Smile, as it will make you approachable. Smiling can help you look less nervous.
- ❑ Remember, everyone else is worried about themselves more than they are about you.
- ❑ Go with someone you know.
- ❑ Practice with others.
- ❑ Remember that you have value to share with others.

- ❏ In the beginning, you may be uncomfortable, but give yourself some time to warm up and feel better in the new environment. The longer you are there, the better you will feel.
- ❏ Prepare questions you will ask the people you meet in advance.

Ask for the Referral

Ask an employee you know at the company you want to work for to submit you as a referral. Most companies offer employees referral bonuses, and amounts range from $250-$1500. Most applicant tracking systems tag referrals; and often times, referrals go to the top of the list. Birds of a feather flock together, and chances are if you are a referral, you'll fit into the company culture if your referral does. I know a company that had metrics in place for their recruiting team for candidates who were referred, one of which was that the recruiter had to review the candidate's resume and take action within 10 days. This shows just how important referrals are to organizations.

Visit www.TalentQ.net/job-search for more tips.

"Alrighty! Next you need to have your Elevator Speech created."

"Can you refresh my memory on what an Elevator Speech is?" Jennifer asked.

"An Elevator Speech is basically a commercial about you. Things you say to pique someone's interest to want to learn more about you. You share information about who you are, what you have done, and highlights from your background. Typically, it should be thirty seconds long but needs to be succinct and stand out so they remember you."

"Okay, where do we start?" She seemed eager.

"We will create your Elevator Speech with the goal of obtaining a new job in mind. Jennifer, answer this question, 'Tell me about yourself?'"

"My name is Jennifer Hanson, I grew up in Shoreview, MN, attended the University of MN for Computer Science, and have been working at North Star since."

"That's a good start. Your Elevator Speech should have flare and personality and include the most important information from your Summary. How about saying something like this: My name is Jennifer Hanson, I'm a data enthusiast who loves helping companies drive revenue thorough analysis and reporting. I collaborate with business leaders to design the reports they need. I won an award from the CIO for my superior participation on a project to redesign data analytics. I graduated from University of MN, I live in Minneapolis, and I have a dog named Daisy."

"That sounds perfect!" she exclaimed.

"If you feel good about it, practice it and commit it to memory."

"I will!"

Create your perfect Elevator Speech below. Here are some reflective questions to ask yourself: How can I explain what I do briefly? What makes me unique? What are some notable accomplishments I've achieved?

_____

_____

_____

_____

_____

_____

_____

_____

CHAPTER 5

I'M PUTTING MYSELF OUT THERE

Avoid the Black Hole of Resumes (It Exists!)

"Somewhere, someone is looking for exactly what you have to offer."

~ Louise Hay ~

"JENNIFER, WHAT COMPANIES have you already applied to?"

"Bark Steel company, and Fiz company."

"Where are you at in the process?"

"Well, I'm not sure… At Bark Steel, I submitted my resume but never heard back. I'm not sure they even received my resume."

"That's not atypical, Jennifer. The black hole exists!" I assured her.

"Darn, I knew it."

"In the past, I worked for one of the largest companies in the US and it wasn't unheard of to have hundreds of people apply to one position. Let me share what is going on behind the scenes with ATS systems, or applicant tracking systems. That is what you used to apply to Bark Steel. When you apply and enter all of your information and upload your resume, it goes into the company's ATS. From there, an internal recruiter for that company is assigned a specific number of requisitions, or what you know as jobs. With the system they use, they can filter the results and eliminate the people who aren't qualified. For example, if the position requires a 4-year degree, they can filter those who do not have a 4-year degree."

"Oh, I see!" Again, the techy in her was excited to hear how this works behind the scenes.

"That's why we updated your resume so it will get a recruiter's attention if you apply on their website. I want to share ways to get around the black hole though."

"Okay."

"We spoke about your network earlier. Do you know anyone in your network who is currently working at Bark Steel?" I continued.

"Ummm, yes, Shelly Crows works there."

"Awesome! How well do you know her?" I asked, hoping she was more than an acquaintance.

"She volunteers at Big Sisters as well," Jennifer added.

"Perfect! I would suggest reaching out to Shelly. Tell her you applied to a position at Bark Steel, send her your updated resume with the job title or numbers associated with the job you applied for on their website, and ask her to submit you as a referral. In addition, ask her who the hiring manager is and if she can email them a short email recommending you for the position with your resume attached."

"Isn't that kind of bold?" she hesitated.

"Jennifer, I know this is pushing you out of your comfort zone, but you need to get uncomfortable to make a change. Remember what we discussed earlier? People will want to help you, I promise!"

"Oh you're right! What do I have to lose?" she smirked.

"Exactly!"

Go Around that Big Hole!
Go around the black hole by utilizing the people in your network. Be bold! Ask them for what you need. Most will want to help you. Plus, if their company has an employee

referral program, referring you may put money in their pocket. Most people will only refer people they believe in, and who will fit into their company's culture.

I'm not discouraging you from applying directly to companies, but the more strategic approach is to have someone you know at the company to vouch for you. When I was in Corporate America, referrals were flagged in the ATS as such and we had a level of service to evaluate their resumes within 10 days. When someone can refer you and recommend you, chances are you'll have better odds landing an interview.

Here is a sample Referral Request letter:

Hello Bob,

I hope you are enjoying this unseasonably warm weather! I sure am!

I'm interested in a position I recently saw posted at your company for a Financial Analyst. The requisition number is TRE0467. This position aligns really well to my skills and career aspirations. I have 7+ years of progressive experience in financial analysis and the qualifications to make me a terrific candidate.

Would you be willing to submit me as an employee referral? I know every open position is highly competitive; and with your help, I understand the chances of being considered would increase. I really appreciate your time and effort.

Please let me know if there is anything I can do for you in return.

Take care,

Jane

Your turn! Write out your Referral Request letters (plural, because you'll need to change important details related to specific positions) and send it to your friends and acquaintances that work at the companies you'd like to work for.

I know it can feel a little — or a lot! — uncomfortable to be bold and ask for referrals, but trust me, people will want to help you!

Visit www.TalentQ.net/job-search for more tips.

CHAPTER 6

I WANT A FIT FOR ME

Search Wisely with Informational Interviews

"Everything you want is on the other side of fear."
~ Jack Canfield ~

"JENNIFER, HAVE YOU experienced an Informational Interview?" I shifted myself to a more comfortable position.

"Let me think...I do remember when I was in college that the career service office encouraged us to do that with companies in which we were interested. They said it was a chance for us to learn more information about companies to really find out if we wanted to work there."

"Yes, Informational Interviews are a great way to learn more about any company. Another objective is to make a great impression on the person you interview so when they have an opening, they will think of you. Knowing people at the companies you want to work for can only benefit you. When you have an Informational Interview, you get to learn about the company from an employee. Plus, in this less formal setting than an interview, the employee is likely to open up more and truly share how they feel about the company."

"I think the career service center at my alma mater arranged the Informational Interview I had previously, so how would I go about doing this now?"

"Great question! There are numerous ways. If you personally know someone at the company of interest to you, you can ask them to introduce you to the person with whom you would like to interview. You could reach out to someone who has a commonality with you, for example, such as an individual who graduated from the same college as you. Lastly, you could reach out to someone you do not know on LinkedIn and request one that way. There are no limits."

"Awesome! Do you think I should meet them in person or via phone?" she asked.

"My recommendation would be to meet them in person. The ideal situation is to meet the employee at their office, so you can see the environment and get a feel for the culture from physically being there. When you are on-site, you can evaluate if people are talking in common areas, and if they are smiling as they walk by. You can assess the vibe when you walk in the door."

"I love that idea!" she exclaimed as she left the office to get to work.

Make a list of companies that interest you and might be a good fit for your next job. You may know people who work there or who previously worked there and enjoyed it. It may be a company who has won awards or recognition for how they do business, how they treat their employees, or for their working environment, volunteer efforts, giving back etc.

Go back through your list and rank them *Most Interested In* to *Least Interested In,* starting with #1. That will allow you to focus your time on obtaining Informational Interviews with the companies on your list. Requesting and setting up these interviews take time. Now start at the one you marked as #1, reach out, and schedule your Informational Interview, and then continue through your list.

Making the Most of Informational Interviews
What questions should you ask during the Informational Interview? First and foremost, ask the questions that will

help you determine if this might be a good fit for you. Refer back to Chapter 1 and ask questions that pertain to those three most important items you are seeking in your next position and employer.

Keep in mind that even though it is an Informational Interview, first impressions are everything. Treat it as if it was an interview so you can be professional and be at your best. After all, you're trying to use an Informational Interview as a way to make a positive impression so that in the future when they have an opening, they will call you first.

Sample Informational Interview questions:

- ❑ When you started at this company, what were the key motivators that led you to join the company?
- ❑ What do you enjoy most about your company?
- ❑ What do you like least about working here?
- ❑ What has been your experience with career development and expanding your skills here?
- ❑ What does a typical day look like?
- ❑ Who do you interact with on a daily basis? How frequent are meetings?
- ❑ What keeps you up at night?

- ❏ What is your strategy for your team for the next year? 3 years out? 5 years out?
- ❏ What are the company's values?
- ❏ How are employees rated on their performance?
- ❏ What are some key characteristics that your company looks for in their employees?
- ❏ How do you celebrate wins or accomplishments?
- ❏ What does the company do to give back to the community?
- ❏ How many employees does the company have?
- ❏ How does the leadership team communicate with the staff?

Visit www.TalentQ.net/job-search for more tips.

CHAPTER 7

I'M READY TO IMPRESS
Nail the Interview

"The difference between ordinary and extraordinary is practice."

~ Vladimir Horowitz ~

I WAS SO thrilled to call her. "Jennifer, I have great news! Alpha Company wants to schedule an interview with you! How exciting!" I couldn't contain my excitement.

"Terrific!!!" Her excitement matched mine.

"Let's walk through what to expect. You will be meeting with three of their leaders simultaneously — the Director of Technology, the Director of Operations, and the HR Manager."

"Okay, how long should I expect to be there?" she asked.

I smiled at her detail-natured question. "Plan on one hour. Have you ever experienced a panel interview before?"

"Yes, but it has been a while."

"No worries, I'll coach you through everything you need to know. When you arrive, ask for Dave. They will bring you to the conference room. The three leaders will ask you to tell them about yourself. This is where you will share your Elevator Speech. Keep it short, succinct, and career focused."

"I'm glad we created my Elevator Speech already," she sighed some relief.

"Yes! Now you get to use it! Next, they will ask you to walk them through your resume. When you are walking them through your resume and background, it is more detailed than an elevator speech. I would highlight your accomplishments in each position and how you were promoted. Some of the other questions they will ask are: *'What makes you frustrated on the job? How do you handle conflict? What are your strengths and what you are working to improve?'*"

Practice is the Key

In order to nail interviews, you need to practice, practice, practice, and practice some more! I cannot emphasize this enough. The majority of the time, the person who lands the job is NOT the person who is the most qualified, highly skilled, with a degree from a pedigreed college; it is the person who interviews the best. The person who *interviews the best* gets the job! This is why practicing is so imperative.

When I say practice, I mean conduct mock interviews with another individual. Have someone ask you questions that you respond to. The ideal situation is to select someone who intimidates you, who will make you feel slightly uncomfortable, and who will give you constructive criticism so you can improve. It also needs to be someone who will keep your interviewing confidential. You should select a few people willing to do a "mock interview" with you.

Interviewing can be a highly stressful experience. Scientifically, the human brain when under stress cannot access memories in our subconscious or long-term memory. To make sure your memories are filed back into your short-term memory, you need to recall them before the interview. And practice, practice, practice is the key to less stress and more access to the information you'll need.

 **ACTION ITEM:**

Write down 3-5 of your top recent accomplishments

1. _____
2. _____
3. _____

Write down how you achieved those accomplishments... not what the team did, what YOU did. Use "I" not "we" when answering.

1. _____
2. _____
3. _____

Write down your top strengths and describe why they are strengths.

Example: I can relate to individuals on all levels. Throughout my career, I have interacted with individual contributors up to C-level executives.

1. _____
2. _____
3. _____

Write down the areas you are working to improve. These should be items that can be seen as strengths.

Example: I have very high expectations. At times, I need to take a step back and realize that not everyone has the same expectations as mine and that is okay.

1. _____
2. _____
3. _____

Write down experiences you had when you successfully dealt with conflict. Perhaps you disagreed with someone. Someone was argumentative. Identify times when you worked with difficult people or had differing ideas.

1. _____
2. _____
3. _____

If you are applying for a position in management, write down 2-3 people you have led and positively impacted, and how you impacted them:

1. _____
2. _____
3. _____

Write down your annual compensation. Knowing how much you currently make is very important. This is your livelihood. How you get a raise is first by knowing what you currently make.

Current Salary: _____

Current Bonus: percentage or amount, how is it calculated? _____

Current Vacation Time Expected: _____

Other Benefits that are Important to You: _____

What do you expect to be compensated for salary?

_____

What do you expect to be compensated for total compensation? _____

What is your high and low number? _____

Standard Questions

What will the interviewers ask? The most common type of questioning interviewers utilize are behavioral-based questions. If you Google "behavioral-based interview questions," you will get a plethora of examples of questions you can answer.

 **ACTION ITEM:**

Google "Behavioral based interview questions," write down ten of them, and answer them in the following 4-step response format:

What the situation was...

What you specifically did...
Speak in terms of "I" not "we."

What the outcome was...
Try to use data in the outcome to make your message more impactful. Know your results and emphasize them with data. Remember, data is more than just dollar amounts — think days, percentages, ratios, rankings etc.

What you learned from it and how you are applying that lesson to current situations...
If you can justify how your salary will be paid by the significant results you can drive to save the company money, you are an asset and they cannot afford to not hire you.

Mindset

If you get nervous during interviews, change your mindset. It is normal to be a little nervous, but your nerves shouldn't get in the way of your interview performance. You have tremendous skills and experience to offer another company. In essence, all you are doing is having a conversation, sharing information back and forth, and experiencing a mutual exchange of information. You are simply sharing the great skills you have and how they could translate and add value to the new company. And the interviewers will share what the company has to offer to you. Don't forget that you are interviewing the company just as much as they are interviewing you. The position and culture has to meet your needs too. At the end of the interview, you need to know that the new company and position meets the needs of the top three things that you determined are most important to you in Chapter 1.

If you know someone at the company, ask them for help preparing for the interview. People want to help others, especially in interviews. If you do not know anyone in advance, ask the representative you have been in contact with for the interviews. Ask them what they recommend for interview attire, what types of questions you should expect, and what the entire interview process looks like. It's in their best interest to help you get hired. They want to help you.

"Jennifer, I want you to wake up in the morning on the day of your interview and have a goal in mind. I want you to say this out loud: *'My goal is to get a job offer from Alpha Company.'* Whether it's the right role for you, you and I can discuss after the interview. Having set this intention puts your mind in the right framework for the interview.

Throughout your interview, you will remember your goal. It will help you present your best self and nail it!" I knew she would nail the interview and I wanted her to know it too.

"I like that suggestion!" she chimed.

"As the interview comes to a close, they will ask you what questions you have. Keep in mind the interviewers are still evaluating you by the questions you ask during and at the end of the interview. Do your research. Check out their website, review the ratings online and, if they are a publicly held company, review their financial results."

I could hear, through the receiver, the sound of pen on paper. Jennifer was taking notes. "Do you get nervous during interviews?" I asked.

"Yes, normally excited and a little nervous."

"I hear you! I get nervous too. Most people are nervous during an interview, so I recommend bringing a portfolio or notebook with the questions you have prepared in advance. After the interview, the interviewer will ask, 'What questions do you have for me?' That is your cue to ask politely, 'I wrote some down in advance. Do you mind if I turn to my notes?' Of course they will say that is fine. Then ask your questions and take notes."

"Oh that's great advice."

Sample Questions to Ask Interviewers

- ❏ What keeps you up at night?
- ❏ What does success look like in this position 30/60/90 days in?
- ❏ Is there anything else I can share with you to feel confident in my candidacy for this position?
- ❏ What is your management style?
- ❏ Would you please give me an overview of your team?
- ❏ How long have you worked here?
- ❏ What keeps you at the company? What is your background?
- ❏ How are employees rated on their performance? And what is the frequency?
- ❏ What does your company provide to employees for continuous learning or career advancement?
- ❏ When you started at this company, what were the key motivators about joining? What do you enjoy most about your company?
- ❏ What do you like least about working here?

- ❏ What has been your experience with career development and expanding your skills here? What does a typical day look like?

- ❏ Who do you interact with on a daily basis? How frequent are meetings?

- ❏ What is your strategy for your team for the next year? 3 years out? 5 years out? What are the company's values?

- ❏ What are some key characteristics your company looks for in their employees? How do you celebrate wins or accomplishments?

- ❏ What does the company do to give back to the community?

- ❏ How many employees does the company have?

- ❏ How does the leadership team communicate with the staff?

Visit www.TalentQ.net/job-search for more tips.

Research the Company

Research the company's website thoroughly in detail. Click on every page. Read through each one. Read about the people there and their leadership team. Google the company as well. Check their ratings on Glassdoor. Review what people have said about the company on Glassdoor, you must take some of this as a grain of salt. Go to LinkedIn and do a search for people who work at the company, evaluate their backgrounds, what type of experience they have, and if they have been promoted?

Doing this research will help you to be able answer these questions: "Why are you interested in working for us?" and "What do you know about our company?" These are two questions that most interviewers will ask.

Phone Interviews

My philosophy is that everyone should ace a phone interview. Yes, you read that right. Everyone should ace a phone interview. If you don't, it is not meant to be.

How can everyone ace a phone interview? Here's how.

You can use the fact they cannot see you to your advantage. Have all your notes laid out in front of you. Everything you did from the previous action items: your accomplishments, strengths, areas for improvement, written out examples of the behavioral based interview questions you researched from Google. Have it all in front of you. You can easily access the information you need. I could almost bet though, through your practice, you have started to memorize all the great things about you!

"Lastly, Jennifer, I need to share Interview 101 tips."

"Sounds basic, Renee." I could hear her smile on the other side of the phone.

"Have a firm handshake, don't chew gum, use good eye contact, exhibit great posture, and don't talk negatively about your current or previous employer. Lastly, don't forget to smile and breathe."

Jennifer laughed, "I can handle that!"

In-Person Interviews

In-person interviews are more comprehensive than phone interviews. They can see your emotions, reactions, and how you interact with others. In-person interviews bring the visual elements to life. First impressions are everything, so I recommend dressing one level above the company's standard dress code. If a company's dress code is casual, I would suggest business casual. If the dress code is business casual, I would suggest professional dress. Personally, I always wear a suit or dress to interviews. This puts me in the most professional frame of mind and, I feel, sets me up for success. Wear what makes you feel comfortable.

I know there are some marketing and technology companies where people won't be hired if they don't wear jeans to the interview. Check with your contact about expected dress code. Have a discussion with them about what you are planning to wear and get their reaction.

Tips for In-Person Interviews

- ❑ Practice your handshake, as you want it to be firm.

- ❑ Use good eye contact. If you are in a panel interview setting, respond by looking at the person who asked the question. Try to include everyone in the room and look at each and every one of them.

- ❑ Do not chew gum.

- ❑ Do not wear perfume or cologne.

- ❑ Mind yourself in the parking lot, as they may be able to see out of the building.

- ❑ Be cordial to everyone you meet, especially the receptionist or security officers, as they will also be evaluating you. Chat with them about the company and share your excitement.

- ❑ Sit up straight and have good posture.

- ❑ Sit at the edge of your chair, as this will make you appear interested and eager.

- ❑ Speak positively about your previous employers.

- ❑ Dress to impress. Wear one step above the expected dress code. Do not wear any clothing that may be distracting. (i.e. showing cleavage, clothing that is covered in cat hair, etc.)

- ❑ Be yourself. If it was meant to be, it will be.

Visit www.TalentQ.net/job-search for more tips.

The Power of References

Arrange a list of references — people you have worked for or worked with in the past. Compliance and policies have driven companies away from checking references, but it's still good to ask people you have worked for in the past if they will be a personal reference. Tell them you want to stand out amongst your competition and having them share detailed information about your previous performance will give you an edge. Pick the people who thought highly of you. Then refresh their memory regarding your accomplishments, providing multiple data points, percentages, hours of work saved from process improvements you made. If they are willing to write a letter of recommendation, bring copies with you.

CHAPTER 8

I'M SHOWING UP AND STANDING OUT
Follow Up After the Interview

*"Your life does not get better by chance,
it gets better by change."*

~ **Jim Rohn** ~

"JENNIFER, I'M SO pleased to hear your interview at Alpha Company went well! That is very exciting!" I smiled when I heard her voice oozing with excitement.

"I know!!! I'm thrilled to have found a company that will treat me like a professional. I really felt like I fit in with the culture and had a connection with the manager."

"Let's reconfirm what is most important to you in your job search. You mentioned you wanted a company that will treat you with respect and as a professional. You also wanted a company where you could learn and advance your skills, and lastly, be paid what you are worth. Sounds like everything is in alignment, right?"

"It really is, and I'm very excited!" I imagined her poised and ready to jump up and down, a far cry from the upset young woman who walked into my office not so long ago.

"Let's do everything we can to make sure they select you as the final candidate."

"Yes!"

"I need you to send Thank You emails to everyone you interviewed with."

"I already started them."

"Excellent! Was there anything in the interview they asked you for which you felt you did not give the best example or response?" I inquired, looking for ways to tie up any loose ends.

"They asked me about a specific time when I had to work cross-functionally. Since I was nervous, I shared an example that wasn't the best example I had. After I left, I was bummed that I shared the example of when I worked across two business units instead of the one that required me to work across four."

"No problem, you can still address that in your Thank You letter."

"Perfect!"

Follow Up with Gratitude

Following up after interviews is an important component of the job searching process. Sending a Thank You email is a critical piece of the interview process. I recommend email versus snail mail. (I'm referring to snail mail as sending a handwritten letter through the mail.) I do not recommend mailing because most companies have made their determination as to who is moving on in the interview process before they even receive your handwritten Thank You letter, unless you overnight it to them. That would be an option.

A well-written Thank You email can boost your candidacy, especially if they are wavering between two candidates. If an employer is wavering between two candidates and you send a Thank You email and the other candidate did not, chances are they will advance you over the candidate who failed to follow up. I also recommend email because you want them to receive your Thank You within 24 hours of the interviews. This shows you are eager, excited, and grateful for the opportunity.

This email should include thanking each interviewer for their time and the privilege of meeting with them, as well as an affirmation of your interest in the company and the position. If you felt a connection to the interviewers, corporate culture, and it satisfies your top 3, ask for the job.

Job searching is like dating. Sometimes both parties hesitate to make the first move. If you express your interest, why you want the job, and how you can add value beyond the stated job description, that will impress them. Think about a candidate who doesn't express the fact they want the job and doesn't state how eager they are to join the team; and they are your competition, interviewing for the same job. You send a Thank You, expressing you want the job and how you can add value to the company, and I can almost guarantee you've just knocked out your competition. We all want a "sure bet," don't we? This also becomes your leverage in compensation negotiations. You are in control. *"I would love to work for you and I'm eager to join your team!"*

Ask for everyone's business cards during your interviews. If they don't have one nearby, ask them for their email and write it down. If you forget this during the interviews, call your contact who arranged the interviews and ask them for everyone's email.

Sample Thank You Email Letter

Dear John,

Thank you for your time and the privilege of having an interview with you on Friday morning to discuss the Financial Analyst position. The rotational program you spoke about seems challenging and rewarding.

I enjoyed our conversation, and learning about your vision for the team moving forward was very exciting. I would welcome an opportunity to be a part of it. I feel my background and personality could add tremendous value to your team and organization.

I look forward to hearing from you regarding your hiring decision. Again, thank you for your time and consideration.

Best regards,
Jane Anderson
612.123.4567
Jane.anderson@gmail.com

Visit www.TalentQ.net/job-search for more tips.

CHAPTER 9

I'M SURE ABOUT WHAT I WANT
Negotiate a Job Offer

"The noblest search is the search for excellence."
~ Lyndon B. Johnson ~

"JENNIFER, I HAVE FANTASTIC news!" I exclaimed as soon as she answered the phone.

"They want to offer me the position?" she asked.

"YES!!!"

"I'm SO THRILLED!!! YES! I never have to be yelled at again!"

"I have even better news, Jennifer. They want to give you a 20% pay increase above your current salary because they value the experience you are bringing to the table."

"NO WAY! That's insane! I'll accept the job!"

Now, I could hear her feet dancing.

Job searching mostly has the hiring company holding the control throughout the process, which can make you feel helpless or stressed. Company representatives control which resumes they review, who they interview, and how much they want to pay you, when you can start, what you'll need to wear, what holidays you get off, and so on.

However, once a company extends you a job offer, the control is transitioned to you. At this point, after a company has extended you a job offer, this is your chance to negotiate any component of the job offer. You are now in control. You know they want you to work for the company. You know they want you to accept the position. This is your chance to ask for what you want. After all, it is YOUR CAREER!

Let me provide some insight into negotiations. If you want to negotiate beyond the initial job offer you are extended, you need to know a few key items. A company who has extended you an offer wants you to join their team and work for them. Companies want people who will accept jobs. No one wants to be left at the altar. If you can tell them exactly what you need to accept the position, chances are they will give it to you. If you can tell them you would accept the position if the salary was X, and you will start on X date, you will have a tremendous amount of leverage at this point.

Perhaps you want more vacation than they initially offered. In that case, you would respond with, "I would love to join your company if I could be given 3 weeks of vacation instead of 2 weeks. If 3 weeks of vacation was granted to me, I could start on X date."

You are in control. With this control, you most likely will get the additional items you requested because they know you will accept. No human being likes rejection. When you eliminate rejection, you're in the driver's seat. Negotiate what you want.

Not sure what salary you should target to negotiate? In my entire recruiting career, it still holds true in most cases that when you are changing companies, you can expect a 10% increase in compensation. For insight on salary averages in your field, check out salary.com and the Bureau of Labor Statistics www.bls.gov. For the Bureau of Labor Statistics, I would use the search field and type, "annual wage and <job title>", for example "annual wage software developer". You will obtain a plethora of information that is accumulated from the US Department of Labor.

CHAPTER 10

I GOT IT

Accepting a Job Offer

"Choose a job you love, and you will never have to work a day in your life."

~ Confucius ~

THIS PHONE CALL was the most important of all.

"Jennifer, now comes another emotional part of job searching — resigning from your current position. I know you have built strong relationships there, however, you will make new ones at your current employer. The people who have become your friends, you will stay in touch with them. They will be very excited for you and your new position!"

"I know it will be bittersweet, but I'm prepared because you made me go through the exercise of writing my resignation letter. It was very difficult at the time. I contemplated if this is what I really wanted to do. Part of me thought I could just stay with my current employer. When I finally broke through and believed I deserved better, I was ready. Thank you for that."

"Oh, of course, my pleasure! Let's walk through what to expect when you resign. You'll meet with your manager privately, tell him you are resigning, and hand him your resignation letter, and you'll feel great about it. A few days will go by, and don't be surprised when your manager asks to have a conversation with you. This will occur after you put in your resignation or may even occur a few days before you are supposed to start with your new employer. He will pull you aside and share how valuable you are to the company, telling you they had plans of promoting you, that they are willing to give you more flexibility, and on and on. You have to remain steadfast on your decision that you've made to leave. Why did it take until you put in your resignation for them to try to correct certain issues? That ship has sailed. They are scrambling because you are an integral part of their team, and they are trying to get you to stay for a stopgap. Most reports show when people accept counter offers, they are no longer employed with their company after six months, whether it is their choice or not."

"Oh really?" she wondered aloud.

"Yes. Let's equate changing jobs to dating. Essentially, you've cheated on your employer by interviewing with another company. How can they ever trust you won't do this again?"

"You're right!"

"Jennifer, keep all of this in mind if this happens to you, okay?" I was doing everything I could to strengthen her resolve and let her know that this is a game that she has to play a certain way in order to win.

"I will. There is nothing they can do to keep me there," she said firmly.

"I had one candidate in the past whose employer doubled her salary in hopes she would stay. She ended up staying. Can you imagine you accept a position with a company, you resign, they call you three days before you are supposed to start and tell you they have changed their mind? When you accept a counter offer, that is what you are doing to them. For people who accept counter offers, chances are they burned the bridge with the company they were really excited about and they will not consider that candidate again in the future."

"Wow! I guess that makes a lot of sense."

"Put in your resignation and I'll stay in very close touch with you before your transition to the new company. Now, it's time to celebrate!!! CONGRATULATIONS, JENNIFER!!!"

CONCLUSION

LOVE YOUR MONDAYS... AND EVERY OTHER DAY

*"There are no secrets to success.
It is the result of preparation, hard work,
and learning from failure."*
~ **Colin Powell** ~

"HELLO, RENEE, IT'S Jennifer!" Her voice was chipper.

"Hey, Jennifer! Great hearing from you! How is Alpha Company?" I could tell by the tone of her voice and couldn't wait to hear the details.

"Oh my gosh! Life changing. I'm incredibly happy! That's the reason for my call. I wanted to thank you for all of your help in finding me this position."

"Oh, I'm so happy for you! It is truly my pleasure, Jennifer!" My heart felt so full.

"They have me working on a brand new project, which shows their confidence in my skills. It makes me feel so good. And remember how I mentioned I dreaded Mondays? Well, now I look forward to them. I'm excited to get back to work on Monday because it's the perfect fit for me."

"I'm thrilled for you!"

As I hung up the phone, I thought about how change is incredibly difficult. As humans, we all strive for consistency. Stepping out of our comfort zones requires a significant amount of energy and can be extremely emotional; and while changing jobs is one of the most emotional changes we can make, getting what we want in a career is very rewarding.

I promise, if you are unhappy in your current position and hate Mondays, there is a better position out there for you. Don't stop looking until you have found it.

Our time here is limited, and I want you to love Mondays too!

Visit www.TalentQ.net/job-search for more tips.

A SPECIAL INVITATION FROM RENEE

Private Access on TalentQ.net to Additional Resources

Ready for more?

Follow the steps listed below to gain exclusive access to even more of Renee Frey's expert advice.

Please send an email to
ihatemondays@talentQ.net

In the subject line:
I'm Ready for More!!

You will receive a password to unlock online bonus materials.

Once you have the password, visit
www.TalentQ.net/job-search
to view the different categories of "extras" available.

ABOUT RENEE

RENEE FREY IS the Founder and President of TalentQ, Inc., an Executive Search Firm that conducts contract staffing and direct hire placements for companies nationwide. As a recruiting expert, speaker, and author, she clears the noise in hiring, making it a positive experience for candidates and clients. She helps candidates land their perfect job and helps companies find top talent.

Her degree in Sociology from the University of Wisconsin, River Falls, combined with 15 years of recruiting experience in a Search Firm and Fortune 500 Company and credential as a Certified Talent Acquisition Strategist, allows her to educate job seekers on real experiences she has had on both sides of the job search with job seekers and hiring leaders. She started TalentQ to create a fresh, positive experience for job seekers and hiring leaders, where she provides full transparency of the process, enlightening everyone she interacts with while she helps companies grow through talent. Her passion for recruiting and her optimistic outlook fuels her in helping candidates change their mindset of job searching from negative to positive.

She resides in Western Wisconsin with her best friend and husband, Dustin, her two daughters, Aubrey and Elena, and her dog, Soleil. She loves boating on the St. Croix and Mississippi Rivers, traveling the globe, and is a red wine enthusiast.

www.ingramcontent.com/pod-product-compliance
Lightning Source LLC
Chambersburg PA
CBHW070259230526
45470CB00002B/640